ANIMAL HABITATS

BATS

AND THEIR HOMES

Deborah Chase Gibson

The Rosen Publishing Group's
PowerKids Press™
New York

Published in 1999 by The Rosen Publishing Group, Inc.
29 East 21st Street, New York, NY 10010

First Edition

Book Design: Kim Sonsky

Photo Credits: Cover, title page, pp. 20-22 © Animals Animals/Stephen Dalton; contents page © Animals Animals/K. Atkinson; p. 5 © Animals Animals/Doug Wechsler; p. 6 © PhotoDisc 1996; p. 7 © Animals Animals/Hans Judy Beste; p. 9 © Animals Animals/Robert Lubeck; p. 10 © Animals Animals/Mickey Gibson; pp. 13, 19 © Animals Animals/Joe McDonald; pp. 14, 15 © Animals Animals/Klaus Uhlenhut; pp. 16, 17 © Richard La Val; p. 18 © Animals Animals/Press-Tige.

Gibson, Deborah Chase.
   Bats and their homes / Deborah Chase Gibson.
     p. cm. — (Animal habitats)
  Includes index.
  Summary: Presents an overview of different kinds of bats and how and where they make their homes.
  ISBN 0-8239-5312-2
  1. Bats—Juvenile literature. 2. Bats—Habitat—Juvenile literature. [1. Bats.] I. Title.
  II. Series: Gibson, Deborah Chase. Animal habitats.
 QL737.C5G53 1998
 599.4—dc21   98-5834
                                            CIP
                                            AC

Manufactured in the United States of America

CONTENTS

BATS OF THE WORLD

Many people think that all bats are the same. But did you know that there are close to 1,000 **species** (SPEE-sheez) of bats in the world? Forty different kinds of bats live in North America alone!

Bats' **habitats** (HA-bih-tats) can be found on every **continent** (KON-tih-nent) except Antarctica. Most bats like to live in **tropical** (TRAH-pih-kul) areas where the weather is warm and mild.

Bats' habitats include forests, deserts, grasslands, and even cities. Bats make their homes in all sorts of places. Trees, caves, houses, and buildings are all places where you might find a bat.

When bats are hanging upside down, they are able to clean their wings by licking them. ▶

WHAT ARE BATS LIKE?

Bats fly, but they aren't birds. Like humans, bats are **mammals** (MA-mulz). Bats have furry bodies and wings with no hair. A bat's wings are really just webbed hands. A bat's wings are similar to a bird's. But bird wings are covered with feathers.

Most bats live to be about fifteen years old. But some have been known to live more than 30 years!

When you are getting ready for bed at night, bats are just waking up. These **nocturnal** (nok-TER-nul) creatures are most active at night. Bats rest during the day. Many of them sleep hanging upside down.

◀ Bats are the only mammals that can fly.

CAVES

Caves make a perfect place for bats to **roost** (ROOST). Caves are quiet and dark. They also have rough surfaces for bats to cling to as they rest. Bats don't usually live alone. Instead, they live with many other bats in a **colony** (KAH-luh-nee). Bats are small, so many bats can live together in one cave.

Bats that live in colder parts of the world have to **hibernate** (HY-bur-nayt) during the winter. This means that in winter, when there isn't much food around, bats rest in one place. The **temperature** (TEMP-ruh-cher) in a cave stays about the same all year round. The heat of the earth around it keeps the cave warm. That's what makes a cave a good place to hibernate and raise baby bats.

A cave, such as this limestone cave in Belize, California, can have thousands of bats roosting in it at once. ▶

INSIDE A BAT CAVE

Each bat cave is its own little world. Millions of bats often cover the ceilings and walls of a single cave. The floor of a bat cave may be covered in a layer of bat waste called **guano** (GWAH-noh). The gases created by guano can make it impossible for other creatures, including humans, to breathe inside a bat cave!

On the Ozark Plateau in Missouri and Arkansas, thousands of Indiana bats spend the winter in the more than 200 caves there. Bracken cave in Texas is home to about 20 million free-tailed bats.

These dawn bats in Bali, Indonesia, may have other caves in which they like to roost besides this one.

HIBERNATION

Bats living in cold **climates** (KLY-mits) are more likely to hibernate than bats whose habitats are warm all year round. Most hibernating bats stay close together to keep each other warm. During hibernation, bats are in a deep sleep. This helps them save energy. Hibernating bats have just enough fat in their bodies to **survive** (sur-VYV) until spring. Then they wake from their rest and hunt for food again.

If bats are disturbed during their hibernation, they waste a lot of energy waking up. Because of this wasted energy, the bat may not survive through the rest of the winter. This is one reason why it is important not to disturb bats when they are hibernating.

Some bats, such as these little brown bats, like to be very close to each other when they're hibernating. ▶

A BAT NURSERY

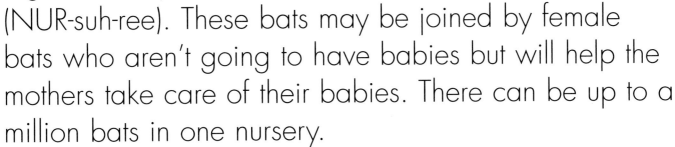

Male and female bats **mate** (MAYT) in the spring. Afterwards, all the female bats who have mated gather together. They all create a **nursery** (NUR-suh-ree). These bats may be joined by female bats who aren't going to have babies but will help the mothers take care of their babies. There can be up to a million bats in one nursery.

Where bats make a nursery depends on what kind of bats they are. Tropical trees make great nurseries for flying fox bats. These bats are fruit eaters and live in warm forests. Insect-eating bats, such as the brown long-eared bat, make their nurseries inside caves or hollow trees. These bats like their nurseries to be warm and quiet.

◀ A mother bat can find her baby in a nursery by the baby's special call and smell.

TREE BATS

Caves aren't the only places that bats live. Bats often squeeze themselves under a piece of loose bark on a tree trunk and roost there. Many bats find homes in hollow trees, or trees with holes in them.

Many tree bats live in warm, tropical climates and don't need to hibernate. These tropical bats use the huge leaves of certain plants as roosts.

The tiny, white-furred fruit bats of Central America make their homes in the huge leaves of the Heliconia plant. They use the leaves like tents to protect themselves from **predators** (PREH-duh-terz) and stormy weather.

These white-furred fruit bats bite palm leaf "fans" to make the leaves fold down into little tents. ▲

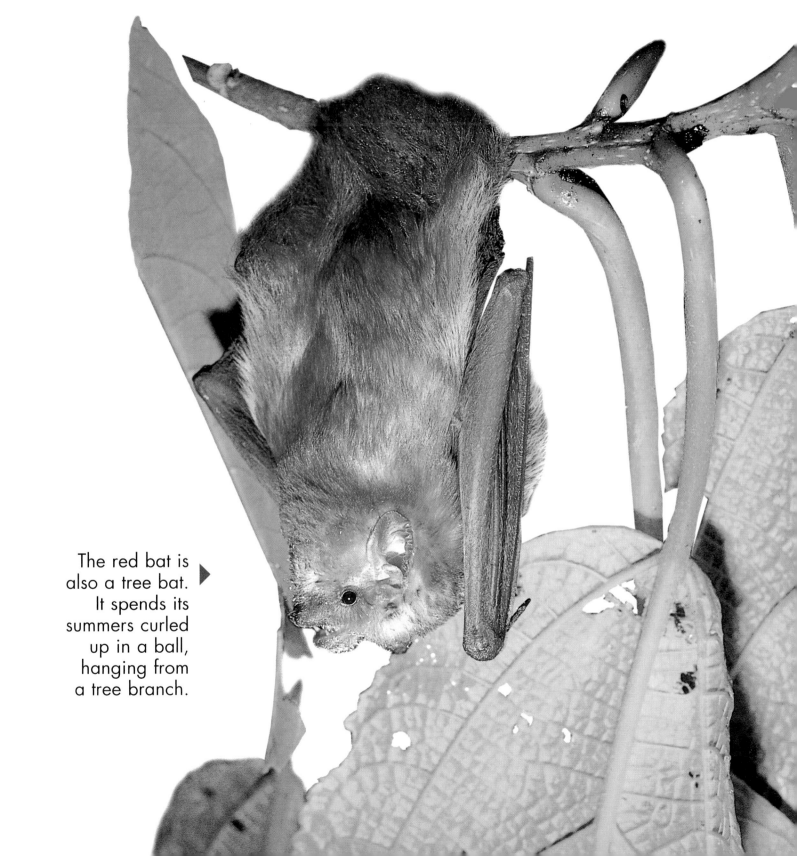

The red bat is also a tree bat. It spends its summers curled up in a ball, hanging from a tree branch.

Bats living in cities need to watch out for cats and rats, which may try to catch and kill bats.

BATS IN THE CITY

As more and more of their natural habitats are destroyed or disturbed, bats have had to find new places to live. Sometimes bats live in cities. They roost under bridges. And some, such as the long-eared bat, even roost in people's attics. When they **migrate** (MY-grayt) a long way from their habitats, bats may use buildings as places to rest along the way.

People all over the world are building special bat houses in their yards or in parks. These simple wood shelters provide a rough surface for bats to cling to while they sleep.

Bats, such as this little brown bat, often live in people's attics. Sometimes they are so quiet that the owners don't know the bats are there.

19

BATS HELP THEIR HABITATS

Having bats around may not sound like a good idea. But certain types of bats actually help other living things in their habitats. The huge **saguaro** (suh-GWAR-oh) cactus of the southwestern United States needs bats to help it make seeds and flowers. The head of the southern long-nose

As bats fly from flower to flower drinking nectar, they bring pollen with them that helps each plant produce fruit and seeds.

bat fits perfectly into the flower of this cactus. After the bat drinks the **nectar** (NEK-tur) of the cactus, he flies off to another cactus, bringing **pollen** (PAH-lin) with him.

These plants need pollen from other plants like them to make fruit and seeds. By carrying the pollen from plant to plant, bats help the plants grow. More plants mean more fruit and nectar for bats.

BATS AND HUMANS

Many species of bats are **endangered** (en-DAYN-jerd) because of humans. People have disturbed so many bat caves that bats can't live in many of them anymore. Many people wrongly fear these animals. Some people think that all bats are vampire bats, which live on the blood of small animals. Others are afraid of illnesses that a bat may carry, such as **rabies** (RAY-beez). Scared people have killed many bats. But bats are no more likely to have rabies than other wild animals. And bats won't attack you unless you do something that scares them.

Scientists study bats all over the world. Knowing more about bats and their habitats will help us find better ways of protecting them.

WEB SITES:

http://www.batcon.org/

http://www.torstar.com/rom/batcave/index.html

GLOSSARY

climate (KLY-mit) The kind of weather a certain place has.

colony (KAH-luh-nee) A group of bats living together.

continent (KON-tih-nent) A very large area of land.

endangered (en-DAYN-jerd) When something is in danger of no longer existing.

guano (GWAH-noh) The body wastes from bats.

habitat (HA-bih-tat) The surroundings where an animal lives.

hibernate (HY-bur-nayt) To sleep through the winter without eating.

mammal (MA-mul) An animal that is warm-blooded, breathes oxygen, and gives birth to live young.

mate (MAYT) A special joining of a male and female body. After mating, the female may have a baby grow inside her body.

migrate (MY-grayt) When large groups of animals or people move from one place to another.

nectar (NEK-tur) A sweet liquid found in flowers.

nocturnal (nok-TER-nul) To be active during the night.

nursery (NUR-suh-ree) A special place where baby bats are born, cared for, and raised.

pollen (PAH-lin) A fine powder that comes from certain flowers and plants.

predator (PREH-duh-ter) An animal that kills other animals for food.

rabies (RAY-beez) A dangerous disease that wild animals can carry.

roost (ROOST) A bar, pole, or perch where bats and birds rest or sleep.

saguaro (suh-GWAR-oh) A huge cactus that grows in the desert.

species (SPEE-sheez) A group of animals that are very much alike.

survive (sur-VYV) To keep living.

temperature (TEMP-ruh-cher) How hot or cold something is.

tropical (TRAH-pih-kul) An area that is very hot and humid.

INDEX